MICROCOSM PUBLISHING is Portland's most diversified publishing house and distributor, with a focus on the colorful, authentic, and empowering. Our books and zines have put your power in your hands since 1996, equipping readers to make positive changes in their lives and in the world around them. Microcosm emphasizes skill-building, showing hidden histories, and fostering creativity through challenging conventional publishing wisdom with books and bookettes about DIY skills, food, bicycling, gender, self-care, and social justice. What was once a distro and record label started by Joe Biel in a drafty bedroom was determined to be *Publishers Weekly*'s fastest-growing publisher of 2022 and #3 in 2023, and is now among the oldest independent publishing houses in Portland, OR, and Cleveland, OH. We are a politically moderate, centrist publisher in a world that has inched to the right for the past 80 years.

Contents

Preface

The Futhark runic alphabet (sometimes referred to as Nordic or Viking runes) is as nuanced and fascinating as it is old. In recent years, many types of divination, alternative spirituality, and old magic in general have enjoyed something of a revival: every major city is likely to have a shop that sells tarot cards, incense, crystals, and the like. Now more than ever, people are looking to the past to try to relearn ancient lessons about themselves and the world using old methods in the face of an increasingly uncertain future.

Runecasting is no exception to this phenomenon. Its simplicity and ability to clearly communicate its message is refreshing and has something to offer for everyone—from folks who have been practicing for decades to folks who have never tried divination but are looking to finally immerse themselves in what it has to offer.

In a lot of ways, this zine is a mirror to my previous title, *A Pocket Guide to Tarot Card Archetypes: When You Don't Want to Carry Around a Library*. I created it as a quick, no-nonsense reference for use when casting Futhark runes. Inside, I'll touch briefly on commonly accepted rune meanings, identify runes that have disputed translations, offer a very short history of the alphabet, and provide several practical methods you can use to attempt your first few castings. Drawing from a number of other published works on the Futhark alphabet (I've listed my favorites at the end of the zine!) as well as my own experience, I've done my best to distill the runes down to their essentials and leave it up to the reader to build their own traditions and interpretations.

A Brief History of the Runes

Futhark runes are very old. The very first runes were thought to have been created between 100 BCE and 100 CE, and our best guess is that they were carved on fallen branches about the size of a finger—hence the most traditional term for a rune being a "runestave."

Their use quickly spread through Germanic and Scandinavian communities, and they continued to be used in some capacity until approximately the early 1800s, giving the alphabet a life of about 1,900 years before it began to fade into obscurity prior to its modern revival. Even after the Futhark alphabet began to be subsumed or replaced by other languages and alphabets, it continued to be used by rural communities and was hugely influential in shaping its successor languages, including what would eventually become modern English.

From the beginning, runes served a dual purpose. Practically speaking, they served as an alphabet of the Elder Futhark language, but they also had a more unique and overtly mystical purpose. Although they could and did form words much like our alphabet, each Futhark rune also represented a separate, distinct word and had a corresponding magical connotation depending on that word. They were also sigils with inherent mystical potential that were said to have been gifted to humanity by the god Odin.

If you were going off to fight, you might have carved Tiwaz (ᛏ) into your club in the hope that it might help you fight a little harder. Or if you were a newlywed hoping for healthy children, you might have whittled a little token of Ingwaz (ᛝ) and kept it in a drawer. Maybe you wanted to ensure that your home stayed safe and warm; you might have carved Othala (ᛟ) on your doorframe.

Three or more runes can also be combined to make pleasingly geometric symbols that are usually referred to as "bindrunes." Bindrunes are said to be stronger together than their individual components and can be as complex as 30 runes or more. Bindrunes aren't covered in this zine, but I encourage you to take a look at them if they are of interest to you. Not only are they inherently powerful, they're also (in my opinion) beautiful.

Regarding the translations of the runes, it's worth nothing that we don't actually have a concrete translation for several runes or that the translation is hotly disputed: primarily Kauna (ᚲ), Pertho (ᛈ), and Algiz (ᛉ). For each of these three, I've used the most commonly accepted translation.

Runes and Their Purpose

As with many other forms of divination, the purpose of casting (or "throwing") runes is twofold: practical and esoteric. Practically speaking, the runes give you a unique way to examine your problems and troubles and hopefully see them in a new perspective. Esoterically speaking, the caster hopes that interpreting the runes correctly might allow them a glimpse into the true nature of the universe: what was, what is, and what has yet to come. This means that there are no bad reasons or times to cast! I'll often cast when I'm feeling especially emotional and I want to try to make sense of it, but many people will cast to see what the week or even that day might have in store for them.

In its most traditional form, runecasting was seen as a way to glimpse into the future, but that doesn't mean that it can't help us look at issues in the here and the now. Someone unfamiliar with runes might be dismayed with how many runes seem to be "negative" compared to some other methods of divination, but this isn't the case. Very few of the runes are entirely good or entirely bad: most of them, like life itself, have a little bit of good and a little bit of bad at the same time.

Picking a Set

Thanks to the modern revival of runecasting, a person can find and enjoy sets of runes that are carved, etched, burned, or otherwise marked into a wide variety of materials, including gems, wood, and even metals. Some are gilded and ornate, while many others simply feature the shape of the rune carved into a token. Oak wood is generally considered the most traditional material, but modern rune sets come in all shapes and sizes.

Many people collect sets and swap out which they use, whereas others find a set that "calls" to them and use that set exclusively. Don't think too hard about it; find a set that satisfies your budget and is appealing enough to you that you'll want to use it. If you're the crafty type (or even if you're not and are comfortable trying something new), I strongly encourage you to make your own! A set that you make yourself might not be as perfect as a set you can buy, but it will be much more satisfying for you to use.

One thing to keep an eye out for is whether the set you're looking at (or making) contains an optional 25th rune: the blank rune. True to its name, the blank rune looks the same as the others of its set except that it has no rune carved into it. We think that the first blank runes started showing up in rune sets at some point in the 1950s and that they are a relatively recent idea. Folks who choose to include it in a set nowadays consider it something of a wildcard; drawing the blank rune indicates an unknown, and the blank rune relies on the other runes pulled during that casting to give it context. The blank rune can also mean that the casting should simply be stopped or that it's been complicated or shouldn't be relied on. The use of the blank rune is entirely up to the practitioner.

Getting into It: The Three Aetts

Elder Futhark consists of 24 runes and was most often broken up into three groups of eight called *aetts*. The name of the alphabet itself—Futhark—is simply a transliteration of the first six letters in the first aett. It's assumed that breaking up the Futhark alphabet made it easier to teach, although some people believe that the three aetts (Freya's Aett, Hagal's Aett, and Tyr's Aett) were intentionally grouped the way that they are and have overt spiritual connotations. Broadly speaking, Freya's Aett is all about the cyclical nature of things (natural and otherwise); Hagal's Aett tends to pertain to external forces that affect us for better or worse; and Tyr's Aett deals with internal factors—things that we use to affect others for better or worse.

Many of the runes correspond to a modern English letter, as the English language borrowed quite a bit from older Germanic languages. However, there are also several runes that have no corresponding letter or that correspond to a letter or sound that modern English doesn't use but that older versions of English did. To cut down on confusion, I've used commonly accepted transliterations for the names of those runes.

The three aetts are as follows, with their corresponding transliterations below:

ᚠ · ᚢ · ᚦ · ᚨ · ᚱ · ᚲ · ᚷ · ᚹ

Fehu, Uruz, Thurisaz, Ansuz, Raido, Kauna, Gebo, Wunjo

ᚺ · ᚾ · ᛁ · ᛃ · ᛇ · ᛈ · ᛉ · ᛊ

Hagalaz, Naudiz, Isaz, Jeraz, Ihwaz, Pertho, Algiz, Sowilo

ᛏ · ᛒ · ᛖ · ᛗ · ᛚ · ᛜ · ᛟ · ᛞ

Tiwaz, Berkanan, Ehwaz, Mannaz, Laguz, Ingwaz, Othala, Dagaz

Without further ado, let's get into meanings and translations!

Freya's Aett

ᚠ

Fehu

Translation: Cattle

Meaning: Abundance, gains, luck, wealth

Fehu can signal some kind of windfall—either physical or emotional—but remember that wealth has its own set of problems to contend with. Wealth might also mean greed, arrogance, or resentment.

ᚢ

Uruz

Translation: Aurochs (a wild ox)

Meaning: Strength, danger, challenges

Like the wild ox, Uruz can signal that there's danger or a challenge ahead—whether to face it head on or try to avoid it is up to you.

ᚦ

Thurisaz

Translation: Giant (the mythological creature)

Meaning: Adversaries, disruption, hostility

Named after the dangerous creatures who often tried to spite the gods in Germanic mythology, Thurisaz is a rune of hostility. A struggle rages, and now is the time to take care of yourself and guard the people in your life.

ᚨ

Ansuz

Translation: God

Meaning: Counsel, inspiration, sacrifice, communication

Not named for any god in particular but rather for gods in general, Ansuz can signal that counsel or communication is needed or that there's sudden inspiration to try to look for. It can also mean that, as might have once been done for the gods, now may be the time to sacrifice something for someone (or something) you love.

ᚱ

Raido

Translation: Journey

Meaning: Momentum, uncertainty, change

Much more esoteric than its sister rune Ehwaz (ᛖ), Raido can signal that you are on or about to embark on a journey (sometimes in the practical sense rather than the spiritual sense!)—and though journeys can mean change, they can also mean hardship. Have you sufficiently prepared?

ᚲ

Kauna (sometimes Kaunan)

Translation: Unknown, but likely "torch"

Meaning: Passion, illumination, destruction

One of the runes whose translation we're not entirely sure of, Kauna's most accepted translation is "torch." And like a torch, Kauna can mean a kindled passion, comforting warmth, or the destruction of reckless fire if misused.

ᚷ

Gebo

Translation: Gifts

Meaning: Recompense, generosity, exchanges

Gebo can signal that now is the time to mend fences. Make up for past wrongs with people you don't like, and give time and energy to those that you do like. Gebo may also signal that a gift is to be received by you instead. It's time to exchange something.

ᚹ

Wunjo

Translation: Joy

Meaning: Community, satisfaction, gains

One of the wholly good runes, Wunjo can signal that brighter times are here and it's time to breathe. Explore passions and find the things in life that can bring you joy regardless of whether life is going perfectly right now.

Hagal's Aett

ᚺ

Hagalaz

Translation: Hail

Meaning: Indifference, painful change, disruption

Hagalaz is an unkind rune, and like the weather phenomenon it's named after, it can signal that painful changes are on the horizon. As with hail, we can't stop it from occurring, but we can do our best to make sure that we're indoors. Hail destroys, but in the end, it also nourishes the land with water.

ᚾ

Naudiz

Translation: Need

Meaning: Constraint, hardship, struggle

In many ways the less fortunate sister rune to Wunjo (ᚹ), Naudiz can signal that there is an unmet need that has gone on for too long and begun to negatively affect you. Look deeply and ask: "What is it that I need right now?"

ᛁ

Isaz

Translation: Ice

Meaning: Stasis, traps, rigidity

Like ice on a road or a lake, Isaz can signal the presence of a trap or other pitfall. Isaz can also point toward stagnation—is there something in your life that you need to approach in a different way? If we are trapped in ice, we have to find a way to break free, and if we encounter it on a walk, we have to cross it carefully.

ᛃ

Jeraz (sometimes Jera)

Translation: Harvesttime

Meaning: Cycles, warmth, reaping

A mostly positive rune, Jeraz can signal that now is the time to reap what you've sown (hopefully something good!) and look to the results of your work—whether regarding work or relationships. Jeraz is also a reminder of the cyclical nature of things—all things eventually pass, good or bad.

ᛇ

Ihwaz

Translation: Yew tree

Meaning: Gateways, life and death, transitions

The yew tree had particular spiritual significance to Germanic peoples: it was a tree with ties to the deceased and the cycle of life and death in general. Ihwaz is, accordingly, a rune of transitions: Look to the people and things in your life that you've lost but also to the people and things you've gained. Do you need to mourn something that you've lost or celebrate something that you're grateful you have?

ᛈ

Pertho

Translation: Unknown, but likely "games"

Meaning: Pleasure, laughter, chance

Pertho is another rune whose true meaning is disputed, but based on its historical context, it is thought to reference gaming and merrymaking and is something of a wildcard. Pertho is a rune of pleasure and laughter, but many games also have an element of chance, and Pertho can signal that a gamble has been made or that something is currently up in the air. Whether the dice land favorably for you or not is yet to be seen. Is there something in your life that you're not certain of?

ᛉ

Algiz

Translation: Elk sedge (a type of prickly plant that is painful to brush against)

Meaning: Protection, safety, insulation

Another rune whose origins are unclear, Algiz is thought to refer to a particularly pointy type of plant that thrives in wet areas. The ultimate rune of protection, Algiz is a good rune: it can signal that someone is watching over you and that whatever dangers you might face will fail to harm you.

ᛊ

Sowilo

Translation: Sun

Meaning: Growth, divinity, wholeness

Like the first rays of sunshine in the spring, Sowilo is a radiant and joyous rune: it can signal help from an outside source, guidance, or a new period of growth. Sowilo can rarely be interpreted in a negative context.

Tyr's Aett

ᛏ

Tiwaz

Translation: Tiwaz

Meaning: Conflict, bravery, promises

Named after a very old Germanic war god (no relation to either Tyr or Thor!), Tiwaz was the "soldier's rune." It can mean that a conflict looms or has already begun and that now is the time to keep your promises and make sure that you emerge unscathed.

ᛒ

Berkanan (sometimes Berkana)

Translation: Birch tree

Meaning: Purification, regrowth

Berkanan is the second tree rune. The birch had connotations of purity, regrowth, and new beginnings. Berkanan can signal that it's time to heal from old trauma and look forward or that something painful or negative has begun to fade away.

ᛖ

Ehwaz

Translation: Horse

Meaning: The sister-rune to Raido (ᚱ), Ehwaz is a friendly rune—like the horse—that can signal the strengthening of partnerships, upcoming travel, and the ability to keep moving in the face of adversity.

ᛗ

Mannaz

Translation: Humanity

Meaning: Compassion, talents, creativity

A complicated rune named after humanity, Mannaz is generally interpreted as a rune of creativity and community: it may be time to create something, whether that's a friendship or a loaf of bread. Humanity is also fickle—ensure that nothing in your life is suffering due to neglect, abuse, or exploitation.

ᛚ

Laguz

Translation: Lake

Meaning: Emotion, the self, looking inward

A placid lake belies its depth; Laguz is the rune of emotions and feelings. Laguz can signal that introspection is needed: Ignore the outside world for a moment and examine your emotional state. How are you feeling about yourself?

ᛝ

Ingwaz (sometimes depicted more traditionally as an upright four-sided "diamond")

Translation: Ingwaz (an old Germanic fertility god)

Meaning: Fertility, closeness, desire

Originally used to bring children and bless newlyweds, Ingwaz is a rune of desire and passion. This might be interpreted in the literal sense, or it might refer to another brightly burning passion that is an important part of right now. Does that passion need to be kindled or controlled?

ᛟ

Othala (sometimes Othila)

Translation: Home

Meaning: Havens, safety, belonging

A rune that was unfortunately co-opted by fascists in the 1930s (an Othala with little "feet" added onto its bottom is called an "odal" and should be avoided at all costs), Othala's true meaning is the home in its purest sense. Othala reminds us that we belong and encourages us to ponder what home means to us and who or where that is. It can also ask us to look at things that have been passed down to us: What have we inherited from our families and the people around us?

ᛞ

Dagaz

Translation: Daylight

Meaning: Insight, hardships ending

Another one of the truly good runes, Dagaz is impossible to misinterpret: like a sunrise, the end of our hardships is just on the horizon as darkness fades behind us. Stay focused and persevere. If things are bad now, remember that they will not be bad forever.

A Basic Runecasting and Other Methods

There are several ways to use your rune set once you've gotten one for yourself, but "casting" runes is the most traditional method and is fairly simple.

Lay down a cloth and mentally pick out three points on the cloth: the center and two points to the left and the right of it that are still on the centerline. There are many cloths made specifically for casting that have markings in these and other areas to help you cast more easily and save you the hassle of picking these locations out yourself every time; I would recommend using or making one if you're able to.

Take all your runes into your cupped hand, give them a thorough shuffling or shaking while you think about your question or problem, and gently drop them onto the cloth from above. Though all of them will hopefully land on the cloth, only three runes matter for this type of casting: the runes that land on your center point, left-of-center point, and right-of-center point. The left rune is relevant to the past or a force in decline; the center rune is relevant to the present or a force in full power; and the right rune is relevant to the future (often the hardest rune to make sense of, understandably) or a force that is on the rise. Remove all but these three runes. Flip them over if they landed facedown, and proceed with your interpretation. If you have runes that overlap or have landed on top of each other, it's up to you to determine which is your left, center, and right rune.

A slightly more modern method mirrors the way that many people utilize a tarot deck: hold the bag of runes and, after shuffling them in the way described above, simply pull three runes from the bag in the order that is most comfortable for you to get them without needing to cast them.

Conclusion

Runes have been around for many years and have brought comfort and protection to the communities that utilized them. Even though our modern world is very different from Iron Age Scandinavia, runes still have a bounty of wisdom for us to examine if we're willing to listen to them. Find your set and find out what they're waiting to teach you about yourself and the things around you, and when you're able, try to help others do the same.

Further Reading

Has this zine piqued your interest and left you wondering what to read next? Great! Consider checking out some of these authors, all of whom offer a deeper dive into runes than I have covered here.

Nordic Runes: Understanding, Casting, and Interpreting the Ancient Viking Oracle **by Paul Rhys Mountfort**

If you can only have one book about Futhark runes, make it this one. Paul Rhys Mountfort offers straightforward translations, nuanced takes on the contested or unclear runes, and plenty of additional supplemental historical information, including folk stories that feature various runes.

The Book of Runes **by Ralph H. Blum**

An immensely popular title on the subject, *The Book of Runes* has been in print for almost 30 years, and for good reason. The text by and large has aged gracefully, though some sections will feel a bit dated compared to a more recent title. You can also find copies that come with a set of runes if you're having trouble picking your own!

Taking Up the Runes: A Complete Guide to Using Runes in Spells, Rituals, Divination, and Magic by Diana L. Paxson

Another older but still very well-referenced rune guide, *Taking Up the Runes* examines Futhark runes from a New Age lens and offers ways to incorporate rune reading into your daily life, including some basic meditations on their meanings.

Futhark: A Handbook of Rune Magic by Edred Thorsson

Futhark is a recently published title that is quite a bit denser than the other titles in this list. I am particularly fond of this one because of how deeply the author examines the meanings of the runes—Thorsson doesn't cover just simple translations and a watchword or two but rather the deep-rooted contextual meanings of runes within the ancient cultures that used them and ways that we can rediscover that knowledge.

PESTS UNITE!
MICROCOSM PUBLISHING.COM